EFFECTIVE ANDROID APP ARCHITECTURE: BEST PRACTICES

BY SYED AHMAD SHAHWAIZ

https://www.linkedin.com/in/ahmadshahwaiz/

Table of contents

Goals and Objectives   3

Why Architecture Matters in Android Development   4

Story About Architecture   4

Maintainability and Scalability   7

Story about Adaptability   11

Testing and Quality Assurance   17

Story about Testing & Quality Assurance   17

Security   22

Significance of security   25

SOLID Principles   28

Story About SOLID Principles   28

What Are the SOLID Principles?   31

Clean Architecture   37

Implementing Clean Architecture with MVVM in Android   40

Layers in Clean Architecture   42

Significance of Clean Architecture in Android   48

Understanding MVVM Architecture   50

Mastering MVI (Model-View-Intent)   55

Comparing MVVM, Clean architecture and MVI   58

Choosing the Right Architecture   62

Final Notes   64

Goals and Objectives

In a bustling world of code and creativity, there exists a book with a noble purpose—to be a guiding light for Android developers of all stripes, from the wide-eyed beginners to the seasoned professionals. This book is on a mission, and its quest is nothing short of remarkable: it aims to illuminate the intricate world of architecture in Android app development.

Picture yourself as a curious explorer, embarking on a journey into the heart of app development. As you turn the pages of this book, it whispers secrets of the trade, urging you to embrace the wisdom of architectural design. It beckons you to construct apps not merely for today but for the distant tomorrows—apps that stand tall, maintainable, scalable, and of uncompromising quality.

This isn't a mere theory-laden tome; it's your trusty companion, ready to traverse the terrain of real-world examples, offering code snippets as trail markers and tales of case studies as ancient scrolls. With these in your arsenal, you'll forge a path through the wilderness of Android architecture, conquering challenges, and sharpening your problem-solving skills.

The world of technology is a tempestuous sea, ever-changing and tumultuous. Fear not, for this book equips you with the knowledge and skills to ride the waves of Android's evolution. It's not just about learning; it's about adapting, about becoming the maestro of Android's symphony, always in tune with the latest trends and innovations.

At its core, this book seeks to unravel the secrets of software architecture. It delves into the very essence of why these principles matter, weaving a tapestry where Android development meets the wisdom of design. As you read on, you'll discover the sacred wisdom hidden within these pages, a treasure trove of knowledge to enrich your journey through the world of Android app development.

Why Architecture Matters in Android Development

Within the realm of Android app creation, creating a visually appealing and functional user interface is just the tip of the iceberg. Behind every successful Android app, there lies a robust and well-thought-out architectural foundation. Android app architecture is not just a buzzword but a critical component that can determine the app's scalability, maintainability, and overall success.

Story About Architecture

Allow me to share with you a tale about a young boy, one that illustrates the significance of architecture in the realm of Android Development.

Once upon a time, there was a young developer named Bazaid. Bazaid loved making Android apps, and he was getting pretty good at it. But as he created more and more apps, they started to get really complicated.

You see, when Bazaid began, his apps were like simple puzzles with just a few pieces. It was easy to change something if he wanted to add a new picture or a cool feature. But as time went on, his apps became like giant, messy jigsaw puzzles with thousands of tiny pieces all mixed up.

This made things tricky. When Bazaid wanted to make a change in one part of his app, he had to be super careful not to accidentally mess up something else. It was a bit like trying to fix a broken toy without making it even more broken.

That's when Bazaid learned about something called "architecture." It was like having a plan, a set of rules that told him how to organise his app's pieces. There were different types of architecture, like Model-View-Controller (MVC), Model-View-Intent (MVI), Model-View-Presenter (MVP), Model-View-ViewModel (MVVM), and Clean Architecture. They acted like special organisers for his jigsaw pieces.

With these architectures, Bazaid could neatly separate different parts of his app, like dividing his toys into different boxes. When he wanted to change something, he only had to look in one box, not the whole messy room. It made fixing things so much easier and less risky.

Imagine if you had a room filled with toys, and each type of toy had its own box. When you wanted to play with or fix a specific type of toy, you just opened that box. No more searching through the mess to find what you needed!

But that wasn't the end of the story. As Bazaid's apps became really popular, more and more people wanted to use them. It was like inviting lots of friends to a party. And guess what? Parties are fun, but they can also get really crowded and chaotic.

So, Bazaid's apps needed to grow and handle more guests (users) without becoming a big mess. That's where architecture helped again. It was like having magic spells to make his app grow gracefully, just like adding more seats to a table without upsetting everything.

With architecture by his side, Bazaid's apps became not only cool but also easy to manage, change, and grow. He could create amazing apps without worrying about things getting messy. And so, Bazaid's journey in the world of Android development continued, with architecture as his trusty friend and guide.

Bazaid's story was not just about one young developer's journey—it was a lesson for all beginners in the magical world of Android app development. With architecture as their ally, they too could embark on their own adventures, creating apps that would stand the test of time and become a part of the digital landscape for years to come.

So, using the right architecture in Android development provides several significant benefits that can help you navigate the ever-changing landscape of technology and ensure your apps remain relevant and adaptable to future challenges and opportunities.

Maintainability and Scalability

In the ever-expanding landscape of Android development, two formidable giants stand guard at the gates of app excellence: Maintainability and Scalability. These guardians hold the keys to unlocking the true potential of your creations, and in this chapter, we shall delve deep into their significance. Let me tell you a simple story to understand this.

A well-structured architecture makes your codebase easier to maintain. As your app evolves and new features are added, you won't need to rewrite large sections of code or risk introducing bugs throughout the application. This maintainability is crucial for keeping your app up to date with changing requirements and technologies.

An effective architecture allows your app to scale gracefully. Whether you're handling increased user loads or expanding your app's capabilities, the right architecture makes it easier to accommodate these changes without compromising performance or stability.

Achieving maintainability and scalability significantly hinges on having code that is modular. Let's delve deeper into this for a closer examination.

Modular Code

Breaking your app's code into smaller, self-contained modules makes it easier to maintain. For instance, separating the user interface (UI) components from the business logic allows you to update or modify each part independently without affecting the others.

Modules promote code reusability. You can develop modules that encapsulate common functionality, such as authentication or networking, and then reuse these modules in multiple parts of your app or even in different projects. This saves time and reduces redundancy.

Modules enable parallel development by allowing multiple team members to work on different parts of the app simultaneously. Each developer or team can be responsible for a specific module, reducing conflicts and speeding up development.

You can test individual modules in isolation, which simplifies the testing process. Unit tests, integration tests, and UI tests can be focused on specific modules, ensuring that changes in one module don't break other parts of the app.

When your app grows, modules make it easier to scale. You can add new features or components by creating new modules and integrating them into your existing app. This scalability is crucial as your app's complexity increases.

Gradle, the build system used in Android development, can take advantage of module-level build caching. This means that changes in one module won't trigger a rebuild of the entire app, resulting in faster build times during development.

Modularisation is a fundamental aspect of dynamic delivery in Android. It allows you to create feature modules that can be downloaded on-demand, reducing the initial app size and improving user experience. This is particularly valuable for large apps or apps with optional features.

Modules enable you to create customised app variants. For example, you can have different product flavours or configurations for different markets or customer segments, all within the same codebase.

Modules help manage dependencies more effectively. You can define module-level dependencies, reducing the risk of dependency conflicts and making it easier to update libraries or components independently.

Modules enforce clear boundaries between different parts of your app. This separation of concerns makes it easier to reason about your app's architecture and helps prevent spaghetti code.

In summary, modularisation is a fundamental practice in Android development that brings numerous benefits in terms of code organisation, maintainability, testability, and collaboration. It's an approach that can lead to a more efficient and scalable development process, ultimately resulting in a higher-quality Android app.

In Android app development, there are several architectural patterns and approaches to choose from, each with its own advantages and suitability for different scenarios. When considering maintainability and scalability, two architectural patterns stand out:

Model-View-ViewModel (MVVM)

MVVM is a widely adopted architecture for Android app development. It promotes separation of concerns, making it easier to maintain and scale your app.

Maintainability: MVVM enforces a clear separation between the UI (View), business logic (ViewModel), and data (Model). This separation makes it easier to modify and extend each part independently. UI components observe changes in the ViewModel, reducing the need for complex callbacks and making UI updates more predictable.

Scalability: MVVM allows for the modularisation of code, which enhances scalability. Different modules can have their own ViewModel instances, and as your app grows, you can add new ViewModels or data sources without affecting the existing parts of your app. MVVM also plays well with other architectural patterns like Clean Architecture, enabling scalability at both the app and data layer.

Clean Architecture

Clean Architecture is a design philosophy that emphasises separation of concerns and layers of abstraction. While it's not a strict architectural pattern like MVVM, it can be implemented alongside other patterns.

Maintainability: Clean Architecture enforces a clear division between the Presentation (UI), Domain (business logic), and Data (data access) layers. This separation facilitates maintainability by isolating changes to specific layers. Changes in the UI or data source do not necessarily impact the core business logic, making it easier to update or replace components.

Scalability: Clean Architecture's layered structure naturally supports scalability. As your app evolves, you can add new features or data sources while keeping the core business logic intact. This flexibility allows your app to adapt to changing requirements and handle increased loads.

It's important to note that there's no one-size-fits-all solution, and the choice between MVVM, Clean Architecture, or other patterns should be based on your app's specific needs and the complexity of your project. You may also consider using libraries and frameworks that align with these architectural patterns, such as Android's ViewModel and LiveData for MVVM or libraries like Hilt for dependency injection and Retrofit for network operations in Clean Architecture.

Ultimately, maintainability and scalability are not solely determined by the architecture you choose but also by the implementation, code organisation, and best practices you follow throughout your Android app development journey.

Story about Adaptability

Once upon a time in the bustling city of Lahore, there lived a programmer named Naila. Naila was passionate about Android development and had been working on creating innovative mobile apps for years. While the city's tech landscape was constantly evolving, Naila had a reputation for building apps that not only met the current trends but also adapted seamlessly to the ever-changing Android ecosystem.

Naila understood that adaptability was the key to success in Android development. Early in their career, she had faced the challenge of apps breaking due to changes in Android versions, screen sizes, and device capabilities. This experience taught her a valuable lesson: to thrive in this dynamic field, one must embrace adaptability.

One sunny morning, Naila received an urgent request from her manager (Tanwir Chaudhry). The client's app, a popular telecom app in the Middle East, was facing compatibility issues with the latest Android update. Users were experiencing crashes and glitches, which had led to a surge in negative reviews and a drop in downloads.

Without hesitation, Naila got to work. They knew that to solve this problem, they needed to adapt the app to the new Android version's requirements. First, they reviewed the app's codebase to identify deprecated methods and outdated libraries. With a clear plan in mind, Naila began the process of updating the app.

They also recognised the importance of maintaining backward compatibility to ensure that the app continued to run smoothly on older Android versions. This meant implementing conditional code blocks and using AndroidX libraries to handle different device configurations.

Throughout the development process, Naila kept a close eye on the Android developer community. She attended meet-ups, read blogs, and actively participated in online forums to stay updated with the latest trends and best practices. This proactive approach helped her anticipate potential issues and implement solutions before they became critical.

After days of hard work and late-night coding sessions, Naila finally had a revamped version of the app. It not only fixed the compatibility issues but also introduced new features that delighted users. The app was now not just adaptable but ahead of the curve.

The client was ecstatic with the results. Not only did their app regain its popularity, but it also received praise for its responsiveness to the latest Android update. As word spread about Naila's ability to adapt and innovate in the fast-paced world of Android development, more clients sought their expertise.

Over the years, Naila continued to thrive in the ever-changing Android landscape. She remained committed to adaptability, always ready to embrace new technologies and challenges. Her story became an inspiration to fellow programmers, a testament to the importance of adaptability in the world of Android development—a world where those who adapt thrive, just like our hero, Naila.

Handling adaptability in Android development involves ensuring that your app can gracefully accommodate changes in the Android ecosystem, such as new OS versions, device types, and emerging technologies.

Here are some best practices to help you achieve adaptability:

1. Follow Material Design Guidelines: Adhere to Google's Material Design guidelines for UI/UX. This ensures that your app's user interface remains consistent and visually appealing across various Android devices and versions.

Example: If you're creating a button in your app, use the recommended elevation, ripple effect, and colour schemes as specified in Material Design guidelines. This ensures that the button looks and behaves consistently across various Android versions and devices.

2. Use Responsive Layouts: Design responsive layouts that adapt to different screen sizes and orientations. Utilise techniques like ConstraintLayout, LinearLayout, and GridLayout to create flexible UIs.

Example: Instead of using fixed pixel values for margins and padding, use relative measurements like "dp" (density-independent pixels) or "sp" (scale-independent pixels) for text. For instance, set margins as "16dp" instead of "16px" to ensure that the spacing adapts to different screen densities.

3. Support Multiple Screen Densities: Provide multiple versions of image assets (drawables) optimised for different screen densities (mdpi, hdpi, xhdpi, xxhdpi, xxxhdpi). This ensures that images appear crisp on various devices. Try to use svg for icons.

Example: When including an image in your app, provide multiple versions of that image tailored for different screen densities. For instance, you can have "ic_logo_mdpi.png," "ic_logo_hdpi.png," "ic_logo_xhdpi.png," and so on to ensure that the logo looks sharp on devices with varying screen densities.

4. Modular Codebase: Organise your code into modular components or features. Modularisation makes it easier to update, replace, or add new features without affecting the entire app.

Example: Suppose you're building an e-commerce app. Create separate modules for product listing, shopping cart, and user profile. If you later decide to update the user profile feature, you can work on the "user profile" module without affecting the rest of the app.

5. Dependency Injection: Use dependency injection frameworks like Dagger or Hilt to manage dependencies. This allows you to swap out components or update libraries without significant code changes.

Example: Use Hilt for dependency injection. Suppose you're using a specific network library in your app. If you decide to switch to another library, you can change the implementation of the network component provided by Hilt without altering the rest of your codebase.

6. API Versioning: Handle API changes gracefully by using versioning in your network requests. Maintain backward compatibility to support older app versions while adopting new features or updates.

Example: When communicating with a backend server, include a version number in your API endpoints. If you introduce changes to the API, maintain backward compatibility by supporting the older version alongside the new one. For instance, /v1/products and /v2/products could coexist to support both old and new app versions.

7. Test on Multiple Devices: Test your app on a range of physical devices and Android versions. Emulators are helpful, but real devices can reveal specific issues related to adaptability.

Example: Before releasing your app, test it on a variety of Android devices, such as phones and tablets with different screen sizes, resolutions, and hardware capabilities. This helps uncover any layout or performance issues that may arise due to device-specific variations.

8. App Throttling: Monitor and optimise your app's performance to prevent battery drain, excessive data usage, or high CPU usage, which can negatively impact adaptability.

Example: Monitor your app's CPU and memory usage using Android Profiler or other performance monitoring tools. Optimise your code to reduce CPU-intensive tasks or minimise network requests to enhance app adaptability and prevent battery drain.

9. Feature Flags: Implement feature flags or toggles to enable or disable specific features dynamically. This allows you to roll out new functionality gradually and test its impact on adaptability.

Example: Implement feature flags using a library like Firebase Remote Config. Let's say you're introducing a new payment method. You can enable this feature gradually for a subset of users to test its functionality and adaptability in a controlled manner.

10. Regularly Update Dependencies: Keep your app's libraries, dependencies, and SDKs up to date. This ensures compatibility with the latest Android versions and access to new features and bug fixes.

Example: Keep your app's libraries up to date. If you're using a popular library for image loading, regularly update it to access performance improvements and bug fixes. This ensures compatibility with the latest Android versions and best practices.

11. Offline Functionality: Implement offline functionality or caching mechanisms where possible. This ensures that your app can continue to work, at least partially, when there's no internet connection.

Example: Suppose you're building a weather app that fetches weather data from a server. Implement local caching of weather data so that users can access previously retrieved data even when they're offline or experiencing a poor network connection.

12. User Feedback: Collect user feedback and monitor app performance. User input can help identify adaptability issues and guide your development efforts.

Example: Incorporate a feedback mechanism in your app that allows users to report issues or provide suggestions. Collect user feedback to identify adaptability challenges and prioritise improvements.

13. Use Android Jetpack: Leverage Android Jetpack components like ViewModel, LiveData, and Room to build robust and maintainable apps. These components simplify data management and enhance adaptability.

Example: Implement ViewModel and LiveData from Android Jetpack to separate UI logic from data handling. This separation enhances the adaptability of your app by simplifying data management and reducing the risk of UI-related issues during updates.

14. Documentation and Knowledge Sharing: Document your app's architecture, coding practices, and known adaptability challenges. Share this knowledge with your team to maintain consistency and make future updates smoother.

Example: Maintain a document that outlines your app's architecture, coding conventions, and known adaptability considerations. Share this document with your development team to ensure everyone is on the same page and follows best practices.

By incorporating these examples and best practices into your Android app development process, you can enhance your app's adaptability and ensure it remains robust and user-friendly in the ever-evolving Android ecosystem.

Testing and Quality Assurance

A solid architecture simplifies the process of testing your app. It allows you to write unit tests, integration tests, and UI tests more effectively. As the Android platform evolves, testing frameworks and tools also evolve, and a good architecture ensures that your testing practices can adapt accordingly. Its time to tell you another story.

Story about Testing & Quality Assurance

In the vibrant city of Riyadh, there lived a software developer named Shahid Rasheed. Shahid was known for his meticulous approach to coding, and he firmly believed in the importance of the right architecture and proper testing. His dedication to these principles was about to be put to the test in an unexpected way.

Shahid had been working on a complex Android app for a startup called "STC" (Software Tech Co.). The app aimed to revolutionise social networking with its unique features and user-friendly design. However, as the project progressed, it became clear that the app's architecture needed some rethinking.

The original architecture was monolithic, with tightly coupled components that made it challenging to test individual features and maintain the codebase efficiently. Shahid knew that to ensure the app's long-term success and maintainability, he had to refactor the architecture.

He began by embracing the principles of clean architecture, modularisation, and the Model-View-ViewModel (MVVM) design pattern. Shahid carefully separated the app into distinct modules, each responsible for specific functionality. This modular approach allowed him to work on different parts of the app independently and made it easier to test each module in isolation.

But Shahid didn't stop there; he knew that having the right architecture was only one piece of the puzzle. Proper testing was equally crucial. He implemented a comprehensive testing strategy, including unit tests, integration tests, and UI tests.

For unit tests, Shahid used JUnit and Mockito to verify that individual components behaved correctly. These tests helped him catch bugs early in the development process, ensuring that each module was reliable and free of defects.

Integration tests were the next step. Shahid used Espresso to create automated UI tests that simulated user interactions within the app. These tests ensured that different modules worked seamlessly together and that critical user flows were error-free.

As Shahid continued to refactor and enhance the app, he faced a significant challenge: ensuring that the changes he made didn't introduce regressions or break existing features. This is where his testing strategy truly shone. With a robust suite of unit and integration tests, he could confidently make changes, knowing that any issues would be detected early in the development cycle.

One day, the section manager of STC (Abdul Majeed) approached Shahid with exciting news. The app was about to be featured on a popular tech news website, which meant a sudden influx of new users. The section manager emphasised the importance of maintaining a flawless user experience during this critical time.

Thanks to Shahid's meticulous architecture and thorough testing, the app's launch was a resounding success. Users raved about its stability and responsiveness. Even with the surge in traffic, the app continued to perform flawlessly.

Shahid's dedication to the right architecture and proper testing had paid off. The app's maintainability had improved significantly, making it easier to add new features and adapt to changing requirements. STC continued to grow, thanks to its robust and reliable foundation.

In the end, Shahid's story became an inspiration to his peers in STC. It demonstrated that with the right architecture and a comprehensive testing strategy, software developers could create apps that not only met user expectations but also thrived in the ever-evolving world of technology.

Now lets see how choosing the right architecture in Android development can impact the testing and quality assurance process.

1. Model-View-ViewModel (MVVM):

In an MVVM architecture, you have a separate ViewModel for a login screen. During testing, you can create unit tests for this ViewModel. You can easily isolate the login logic, such as validating credentials and handling login states, within the ViewModel. This separation simplifies testing, as you can verify the ViewModel's behaviour independently of the UI components, ensuring that the login functionality works correctly.

2. Clean Architecture:

Suppose you're developing a weather app. With Clean Architecture, you can separate the core business logic (use cases) from external dependencies (data sources). During testing, you can write unit tests for use cases like "GetWeatherForecastUseCase." These tests can validate how the use case processes data and ensures that it produces accurate weather forecasts regardless of the underlying data source (e.g., network or local database).

3. Modularisation:

Your e-commerce app has multiple features like product listing, cart management, and user profiles. Using a modular architecture, each feature is encapsulated within its module. This modularity allows you to create focused test suites for individual features. For instance, you can write unit tests for the "CartManager" module to ensure that it handles cart operations correctly without affecting the product listing or user profile features.

4. Dependency Injection:

Let's say you're building a messaging app that relies on a network service for sending and receiving messages. By implementing dependency injection with Dagger or Hilt, you can inject mock network services during testing. This allows you to simulate various network scenarios, such as slow connections or server errors, to ensure that your app handles these situations gracefully.

5. Android Jetpack Components:

You're developing a news reader app using Android Jetpack's ViewModel and LiveData. The ViewModel is responsible for fetching and managing news data. During testing, you can create unit tests for the ViewModel, mocking the data source (e.g., a remote API or local database). This approach allows you to verify that the ViewModel correctly handles data retrieval, transformation, and updates, ensuring a reliable news reading experience.

6. MVP (Model-View-Presenter):

In an MVP architecture, consider a calculator app. The Presenter contains the business logic for performing calculations, while the View handles the UI. During testing, you can write unit tests for the Presenter, validating its ability to perform calculations accurately and handle user input effectively. The clear separation between the View and Presenter makes it straightforward to test the core functionality.

7. Modular Package Structure:

Your ride-sharing app consists of several modules, including ride booking, payment processing, and driver tracking. With a modular package structure, each module is organised into its package hierarchy. This structure simplifies testing, as you can focus on testing one module at a time. For instance, you can write unit tests specifically for the payment processing module to ensure secure and reliable payment transactions.

8. Continuous Integration and Continuous Delivery (CI/CD):

Consider a news app with modules for news articles, comments, and user profiles. Each module is encapsulated within a feature module, making it suitable for CI/CD integration. Your CI/CD pipeline can run dedicated tests for each feature module, ensuring that changes in one module do not break functionality in others. This modular structure enables parallel testing, speeding up the overall testing process and promoting a faster release cycle.

Incorporating these examples into your Android development workflow demonstrates how architectural choices can significantly impact the effectiveness of testing and quality assurance efforts. A well-thought-out architecture not only enhances the reliability of your app but also streamlines the testing process, enabling you to deliver a high-quality product to your users.

Security

Choosing the right architecture for your Android app can have a significant impact on its security. Security is a critical aspect of app development, and the architectural decisions you make can either enhance or compromise the security of your application. Story About Security

This is a story of a boy named Nauman who lived in Lahore. Nauman had a passion for technology and always dreamed of becoming a renowned Android app developer.

As Nauman's skills grew, so did his ambitions. He decided to build a mobile banking app, named "SafeBank," that would allow users to manage their finances securely. He knew that security was paramount for such an app, and he was determined to make it impervious to threats and vulnerabilities.

One sunny afternoon, while sipping on a glass of Rabri, Nauman embarked on his journey to create SafeBank. He understood that choosing the right architecture was crucial for ensuring the security of his app.

The Foundation of Security

Nauman began his quest by selecting a solid architectural foundation for SafeBank. He opted for Clean Architecture, a well-structured approach that emphasised separation of concerns. This architectural choice allowed him to isolate sensitive financial data and security-related logic from the user interface.

Within this architecture, he created a secure vault for storing secret API keys and encryption keys. These keys were protected with the latest encryption algorithms, making them virtually impenetrable to prying eyes. Only authorised components of the app had access to these keys, ensuring that data remained confidential.

Building Strong Defences

With Clean Architecture in place, Nauman started building the app's core security features. He implemented robust encryption mechanisms to safeguard user data, ensuring that all sensitive information, such as account numbers and transaction history, remained encrypted both in transit and at rest. The use of strong encryption algorithms, coupled with secure key management, made it nearly impossible for attackers to intercept or decrypt sensitive data.

The Guardian of Authentication

For authentication, Nauman adopted the Model-View-ViewModel (MVVM) pattern. He implemented secure authentication flows, such as biometric authentication and multi-factor authentication, using Android's built-in security features. This ensured that only authorised users could access the app, even if their devices fell into the wrong hands.

The Watchful Eye of Testing

Nauman knew that thorough testing was essential for detecting security vulnerabilities. He diligently wrote unit tests and instrumented tests, simulating various attack scenarios, such as data tampering and injection attacks. Clean Architecture made it easy to test the app's security features in isolation.

To further protect the app's codebase from reverse engineering and tampering, Nauman employed DexGuard, an advanced Android obfuscation and encryption tool. DexGuard scrambled the bytecode, making it extremely challenging for attackers to decompile or modify the app.

Fortifying the Backend

SafeBank relied on a robust backend server to handle transactions and account management. Nauman collaborated with backend developers to implement secure API endpoints, employing industry-standard authentication and authorisation mechanisms. Additionally, communication between the app and the server was encrypted using secure protocols, ensuring that data remained confidential during transit.

Regular Vigilance

As SafeBank took shape, Nauman understood that security was an ongoing concern. He remained vigilant, keeping the app and its dependencies up-to-date with the latest security patches and libraries. Regular security audits and penetration tests helped identify and rectify any vulnerabilities.

The Happy Ending

SafeBank was finally ready to launch, and Nauman's hard work had paid off. Users embraced the app for its sleek design and, most importantly, its unwavering commitment to security. Thanks to the right architectural choices, robust encryption, secret key management, DexGuard protection, and diligent testing, the app withstood security audits and penetration tests, earning the trust of its users.

And so, Nauman Bhatti, not only fulfilled his dream of becoming a renowned Android app developer but also created a secure and reliable mobile banking app that helped people manage their finances with confidence. The story of SafeBank demonstrated that choosing the right architecture and implementing advanced security measures were not just about building an app; they were about building trust and ensuring the safety of users' financial journeys in the digital world.

Significance of security

Here's how security is affected by choosing the right architecture:

1. Separation of Concerns (SoC):

Example: In a Clean Architecture-based Android app, the business logic for user authentication is kept separate from the UI layer. The "use case" or "interactor" responsible for user authentication is a distinct component. This separation ensures that security-related code (like hashing passwords or verifying tokens) is confined to a well-defined module, making it easier to manage and update security measures without affecting the UI layer. Additionally, DexGuard is used to obfuscate the bytecode, making it more challenging for potential attackers to reverse engineer and extract sensitive security algorithms.

2. Modularisation:

Example: An e-commerce app might have a dedicated "Payment" module responsible for processing payments securely. This module can encapsulate payment gateway integration, encryption of payment data, and handling of payment-related errors. By isolating payment processing in this module, you minimise the risk of security issues affecting other parts of the app. DexGuard's code obfuscation techniques are applied to this module to further obscure the payment processing logic, making reverse engineering attempts less fruitful.

3. Code Isolation:

Example: In a healthcare app, patient medical records are highly sensitive. These records can be stored and managed within a dedicated "Medical Records" module. This module enforces strict access controls and encryption, preventing unauthorised access or tampering with patient data from other parts of the app. Additionally, DexGuard is employed to protect the encryption and access control mechanisms, making it harder for attackers to analyse and exploit vulnerabilities.

4. Dependency Injection:

Example: Using HILT for dependency injection, you can securely provide cryptography-related dependencies to the parts of your app that require them. For instance, you can inject cryptographic libraries and configurations into modules responsible for data encryption, ensuring that sensitive data is processed using trusted components. DexGuard is used to obfuscate Dagger's generated code, making it more resistant to reverse engineering and tampering.

5. Testing:

Example: A banking app employs extensive security testing. Unit tests are written to verify that encryption and decryption functions work correctly. Integration tests simulate various security scenarios, such as login attempts with incorrect credentials, to ensure that security measures effectively protect user accounts and data. Additionally, DexGuard is used to protect the testing codebase, preventing attackers from analyzing the app's security test cases to identify weaknesses.

6. Data Encryption:

Example: In a messaging app, all messages are end-to-end encrypted using the Signal Protocol. The encryption and decryption logic are encapsulated within a dedicated "Encryption" module, ensuring that sensitive messages are secure from eavesdropping and unauthorised access. DexGuard is applied to this module to protect the encryption algorithms and key management, making it extremely challenging for attackers to reverse engineer the encryption implementation.

7. Access Control:

Example: A document management app employs role-based access control (RBAC). Users are assigned roles (e.g., "Admin," "Editor," "Viewer"), and access to documents is determined by their roles. The architecture enforces access control policies, ensuring that users can only perform actions allowed by their roles. DexGuard is used to protect the RBAC logic, making it more resilient against reverse engineering attempts aimed at circumventing access controls.

8. Secure Communication:

Example: An online banking app uses SSL/TLS to establish secure connections with its backend servers. It also implements certificate pinning to validate server certificates, preventing man-in-the-middle attacks and ensuring that communication remains confidential and secure. DexGuard is used to protect the certificate pinning logic and SSL/TLS implementation, making it difficult for attackers to intercept and manipulate network traffic.

9. Security Updates:

Example: A mobile security app frequently releases updates to address newly discovered vulnerabilities. The app's architecture allows for easy updates to the vulnerability scanning engine, ensuring that users receive timely security patches to protect their devices from emerging threats.

10. Compliance:

Example: An app handling personal health information (PHI) complies with the Health Insurance Portability and Accountability Act (HIPAA). The architecture enforces strict data encryption, access controls, and audit trails to meet HIPAA's requirements for protecting patient privacy and data security.

These examples illustrate how choosing the right architecture and applying security principles can address specific security concerns in Android app development. Each architectural decision aligns with a security best practice, contributing to a more secure and robust application.

SOLID Principles

In the ever-evolving landscape of software development, crafting high-quality, maintainable, and scalable code is paramount. Achieving this goal often requires adherence to established best practices and principles. Among these, the SOLID principles stand as pillars of sound object-oriented design and software architecture. These principles provide a blueprint for developers to create robust and flexible software systems. In this chapter, we will delve into the significance of the SOLID principles and how they empower developers to build better software.

But before diving into the SOLID principles, guess what? Its story time.

Story About SOLID Principles

In a spooky old software company, there was something strange happening. The developers talked in hushed tones about something mysterious that was affecting their work. It was the SOLID principles, and they were causing some eerie things to occur.

It all started when a smart but strange developer named Alzuwayyid took charge of a software project. Alzuwayyid was very focused on keeping code clean and organised. He talked about the SOLID principles as if they were magical rules.

Alzuwayyid's first move was to apply the Single Responsibility Principle (SRP). He began breaking the big, messy code into lots of tiny pieces, each with its own job. The developers watched as the code changed, and it was fascinating and scary at the same time.

But as the project went on, weird stuff began to happen. Late at night, developers claimed they could hear voices coming from the code. The voices whispered things like, "I have one job, and I'll do it no matter what." It was as if the code had a mind of its own and was determined to follow SRP at any cost.

The code became stubborn. It refused to work with any changes that didn't fit its one job. When developers tried to add new features, the code would say, "That's not my job!" It was like the code was alive and didn't want to do anything else.

As the project continued, Alzuwayyid introduced the Open-Closed Principle (OCP). He wanted to make sure that existing code didn't change, but you could add new things to it. The code became a maze of abstract classes and interfaces, and it felt impossible to understand.

With OCP in place, the code got even stranger. Developers found they couldn't change existing code anymore. If they tried, the code would throw errors and refuse to work, saying it was closed for changes. They had to use complex tricks to add new stuff, and the code became a mess.

Then came the Liskov Substitution Principle (LSP). Code that used to be simple became complicated with lots of new classes. If you didn't do things exactly right, the code would show weird errors, and it was hard to figure out what was wrong.

The Interface Segregation Principle (ISP) was the scariest. If you implemented unnecessary stuff from an interface, the code would add things you didn't want. It was like a ghost changing your code, and it made things very confusing.

Finally, the Dependency Inversion Principle (DIP) caused trouble. Alzuwayyid used special containers that did things on their own. They added dependencies that nobody wanted, and the code started crashing. It was like a bad dream.

The developers were stuck. They couldn't escape the strange rules of the SOLID principles. Alzuwayyid disappeared, leaving them with a spooky codebase that followed strange rules and acted in mysterious ways.

However, as time went on, they began to realise that there was a way to harness the power of SOLID for good and bring a happy ending to their software development journey.

At first, the codebase had become a tangled mess of small, single-responsibility classes, abstract interfaces, and complex inheritance hierarchies. It seemed as though the code had a mind of its own, enforcing strict rules at every turn. But the developers were determined to master these principles rather than be haunted by them.

They decided to embrace the Single Responsibility Principle (SRP) wholeheartedly. Each class had its own clear purpose, and the developers found that this made the code easier to read and understand. Bugs were reduced, and the team's productivity increased as they could focus on one thing at a time.

With the Open-Closed Principle (OCP), the developers learned to create flexible and extensible code. They leveraged interfaces and abstract classes to allow for easy extension while keeping existing code intact. This meant that adding new features became a breeze, and the codebase evolved gracefully over time.

The Liskov Substitution Principle (LSP) was no longer a source of fear. Developers became experts at creating derived classes that adhered to the contracts of their parent classes. This made the code more predictable and reliable, and the team could trust that their changes wouldn't introduce unexpected issues.

The Interface Segregation Principle (ISP) was applied sensibly. Interfaces were designed to be small and focused, ensuring that clients only implemented what they needed. This reduced unnecessary dependencies and made the codebase more adaptable to change.

Finally, the Dependency Inversion Principle (DIP) became a cornerstone of their architecture. Dependency injection and inversion of control containers were used to manage dependencies seamlessly. This led to a codebase that was decoupled and modular, making it easier to test and maintain.

As the developers embraced and mastered the SOLID principles, their codebase underwent a transformation. It became a model of clarity, adaptability, and maintainability. Bugs became a rarity, and new features were added with ease. The team's morale soared as they worked with code that was no longer a source of dread.

Alzuwayyid, the developer who had introduced the SOLID principles, returned to see the remarkable progress his team had made. He was pleased to see that they had not only conquered the challenges of SOLID but had also embraced its benefits.

In the end, the developers and Alzuwayyid celebrated their success. The SOLID principles had gone from being a source of mystery and fear to a set of guiding principles that led them to software development bliss. Their codebase was now a shining example of how SOLID could bring order and happiness to the world of software development. And so, in this happy ending, the team proved that with dedication and understanding, even the most challenging principles can lead to software development success.

The previous story provided insights into the consequences of incorrectly applying solid principles, illustrating that it can lead to challenging situations. However, when solid principles are comprehensively understood and their use-cases are clear, they can transform your codebase into something truly remarkable.

What Are the SOLID Principles?

The SOLID principles are a set of five design principles, initially introduced by Robert C. Martin, also known as Uncle Bob. They are as follows:

Single Responsibility Principle (SRP): A class should have only one reason to change, meaning it should have a single responsibility or function. This principle encourages code to be more focused and easier to maintain.

For example a class responsible for database access should focus solely on database operations, while a separate class handles user authentication.

Problem: A class or module should have only one reason to change. When it has multiple responsibilities, changes in one area may inadvertently affect other areas.

Example: Consider a "User" class that not only manages user data but also handles authentication. Implementing SRP, you'd split this into separate "User" and "Authentication" classes. This way, changes to authentication logic won't impact user data management and vice versa.

Open-Closed Principle (OCP): Software entities (classes, modules, functions) should be open for extension but closed for modification. This encourages the use of abstractions and inheritance to allow new functionality to be added without altering existing code.

For instance, you can create new subclasses or implementations to extend functionality while keeping the base code untouched.

Problem: Software entities (e.g., classes, modules) should be open for extension but closed for modification. You should be able to add new functionality without altering existing code.

Example: Imagine a drawing application with shapes like circles and rectangles. Instead of modifying the existing "Shape" class every time you add a new shape, you create new shape classes that extend an abstract "Shape" class. This adheres to OCP as it allows you to add new shapes without changing existing code.

Liskov Substitution Principle (LSP): Subtypes must be substitutable for their base types without affecting the correctness of the program. This principle ensures that derived classes maintain the expected behaviour of their parent classes.

For instance, if you have a Bird class, a subclass like Penguin should be able to replace Bird without causing issues.

Problem: Software entities (e.g., classes, modules) should be open for extension but closed for modification. You should be able to add new functionality without altering existing code.

Example: Imagine a drawing application with shapes like circles and rectangles. Instead of modifying the existing "Shape" class every time you add a new shape, you create new shape classes that extend an abstract

"Shape" class. This adheres to OCP as it allows you to add new shapes without changing existing code.

Interface Segregation Principle (ISP): Clients should not be forced to depend on interfaces they do not use. This principle promotes the creation of smaller, more specific interfaces rather than large, monolithic ones.

In practice, this means creating smaller and more specific interfaces rather than large, monolithic ones. This allows clients to implement only the methods they need, preventing unnecessary dependencies.

Problem: Clients should not be forced to depend on interfaces they don't use. Large interfaces with many methods can lead to unnecessary dependencies and make classes implement methods they don't need.

Example: If you have an "Employee" interface with methods like "calculatePay" and "assignProject," consider splitting it into smaller interfaces like "Payable" and "Assignable." This allows classes to implement only the interfaces relevant to their functionality.

Dependency Inversion Principle (DIP): High-level modules should not depend on low-level modules; both should depend on abstractions. This principle encourages the use of dependency injection and inversion of control to achieve decoupling and flexibility.

For instance, instead of directly depending on a specific database library, you depend on an abstract database interface, making it easier to switch to a different database implementation.

Problem: High-level modules should not depend on low-level modules; both should depend on abstractions. Abstractions should not depend on details; details should depend on abstractions.

Example: In a messaging app, instead of directly calling a specific messaging service, you create an abstract messaging interface and concrete implementations for various services (e.g., SMS, Email). High-level modules (e.g., the user interface) depend on the abstract interface, allowing you to switch between messaging services without modifying the UI code.

Applying these SOLID principles in your codebase can lead to more maintainable, flexible, and easily extendable software, making it easier to adapt to changing requirements and scale your application.

The SOLID principles of object-oriented design

While all five share inherent and co-dependent relationships, each one of the SOLID principles involves its own scope of concepts and practices.

Single responsibility	**Open/closed**	**Liskov substitution**	**Interface segregation**	**Dependency inversion**
An object class should only be responsible for one specific function, and only have one reason to change.	Developers should be able to add new features, functions and extensions to a class while leaving the rest of the existing codebase intact.	The objects contained in a subclass must exhibit the same behavior as any higher-level superclass it's dependent on.	Create a separate client interface for each class within an application, even if those classes share some of the same methods (or similar methods).	When a subclass is dependent on a superior class, the higher-level class should not be affected by any changes made to the subclass.

The Significance of SOLID Principles

Code Maintainability: The SOLID principles emphasise code organisation and separation of concerns. By adhering to these principles, developers create code that is easier to understand, update, and maintain. When changes are required, developers can confidently modify specific parts of the codebase without affecting unrelated areas.

Scalability: SOLID principles promote modular and flexible code. This modularity allows developers to extend and scale their software systems efficiently. As new features or requirements arise, developers can introduce new modules or classes without needing to rewrite existing code.

Testability: SOLID code is inherently more testable. The principles encourage the use of interfaces, abstractions, and dependency injection, which make it simpler to write unit tests and ensure that individual components of the software function correctly.

Code Reusability: The SOLID principles foster code reusability. By adhering to these principles, developers create classes and modules that are self-contained and can be reused in different parts of an application or in entirely separate projects.

Reduced Bugs and Defects: SOLID principles help minimise bugs and defects by encouraging clean, well-structured code. The principles prevent common issues like tight coupling, which can lead to unintended side effects and errors in the codebase.

Enhanced Collaboration: When developers follow SOLID principles, it becomes easier for teams to collaborate. The principles provide clear guidelines for code structure and organisation, making code reviews and collaborative development more efficient.

Adaptability to Change: SOLID code is adaptable to change. As software requirements evolve or new technologies emerge, SOLID principles provide a foundation that allows developers to make updates and additions with confidence, knowing that existing functionality remains intact.

Clean Architecture

One architectural paradigm that has gained significant traction in recent years is Clean Architecture. In this chapter, we'll delve into what Clean Architecture is, why it's crucial for Android app development, and how it can empower you to create highly maintainable, scalable, and testable Android apps.

Clean Architecture is a software design concept and architectural pattern that has been popularised by Robert C. Martin, also known as "Uncle Bob." Robert C. Martin is a well-known software engineer, author, and speaker, and he introduced the concept of Clean Architecture as part of his broader Clean Code movement.

Clean Architecture emphasises the separation of concerns and the organisation of code in a way that promotes maintainability, testability, and adaptability. It provides a structured approach to software development that aims to minimise dependencies on external frameworks and technologies, ensuring that the core business logic remains independent and isolated from external concerns.

While Clean Architecture has its roots in Robert C. Martin's work, it has been adopted and adapted by the software development community at large, including Android development. Many developers and organisations have embraced Clean Architecture as a best practice for building robust and maintainable software applications in various domains.

Story about clean architecture

There lived a passionate Android app developer named Mughees Musaddiq. Mughees had a vision of creating the most remarkable weather app ever seen in the Play Store. But he knew that building a top-notch app required more than just writing code; it demanded a rock-solid architectural foundation.

Mughees had heard about Clean Architecture, a design philosophy that promised to revolutionise the way Android apps were developed. Intrigued by the possibilities, he decided to embark on a journey to implement Clean Architecture in his weather app.

Chapter 1: The Conundrum

As Mughees started coding his weather app, he encountered a common challenge faced by many developers—the codebase was growing rapidly, and it was becoming increasingly difficult to manage. Bugs seemed to appear out of nowhere, and making changes to one part of the app often led to unintended consequences in other areas.

Determined to bring order to the chaos, Mughees decided to implement Clean Architecture.

Chapter 2: The Layers Unveiled

Mughees began by dividing his app into three distinct layers:

The Data Layer: This layer was responsible for fetching weather data from external sources like APIs and databases. Mughees created repositories to abstract data access and separate it from the rest of the app.

The Domain Layer: At the core of his architecture, the domain layer contained the business logic for the weather app. Here, Mughees defined entities representing weather data and implemented use cases for handling weather-related operations.

The Presentation Layer: This was where the user interface resided. Mughees designed activities, fragments, and view models to display weather information and handle user interactions. The presentation layer communicated with the domain layer to fetch and display data.

Chapter 3: The Benefits Unleashed

As Mughees implemented Clean Architecture, he started to notice remarkable improvements in his weather app:

Maintainability: With a clear separation of concerns, making changes to one layer didn't disrupt the others. Mughees could update the user interface or change data sources without rewriting the entire app.

Testability: The domain layer, free from Android-specific dependencies, became highly testable. Mughees could write unit tests to ensure the core logic functioned flawlessly.

Flexibility: When the weather app gained popularity, Mughees was able to add new features and even integrate additional weather data sources with ease. Clean Architecture allowed him to scale the app gracefully.

Chapter 4: The Happy Ending

Mughees's weather app, built on Clean Architecture principles, became a sensation in Lahore. Users marvelled at its reliability, beautiful UI, and the accuracy of weather information. Mughees continued to evolve the app, adapting to new weather data providers and embracing the latest Android technologies.

Clean Architecture had not only improved the quality and maintainability of his code but also empowered him to create a truly remarkable Android app. Mughees's journey with Clean Architecture was a testament to the power of a well-structured architectural foundation in the world of Android app development.

And so, in the heart of Lahore, Mughees Musaddiq's story became an inspiration for fellow developers, reminding them that with Clean Architecture, they could turn their app dreams into reality, one well-structured layer at a time.

Implementing Clean Architecture with MVVM in Android

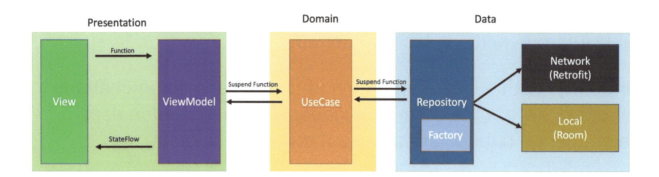

In Clean Architecture for Android, the architecture typically consists of three main layers: the data layer, the domain layer, and the presentation layer. These layers are organised in a hierarchical manner, with each layer having distinct responsibilities and dependencies, as follows:

Data Layer: This is the outermost layer and deals with data-related concerns. It includes components responsible for interacting with external data sources and storage mechanisms, such as databases and APIs. Key components in the data layer include repositories, data sources, and mappers. The data layer is responsible for retrieving, storing, and transforming data.

Domain Layer: The domain layer, also known as the business logic layer, resides at the core of the architecture. It encapsulates the core business rules, entities, and use cases (interactors) that define the application's functionality. The domain layer is agnostic of external frameworks, databases, or user interfaces and focuses solely on the business logic.

Presentation Layer: This is the innermost layer responsible for handling the user interface (UI) and user interaction aspects of the application. It includes UI components, such as activities, fragments, view models, and presenters, which are responsible for rendering data to the user's screen and capturing user input. The presentation layer communicates with the domain layer to access business logic and data.

These three layers form a clear separation of concerns, with data-related operations and interactions with external systems residing in the data layer, core business logic residing in the domain layer, and user interface and interaction handling in the presentation layer. The primary goal of Clean Architecture is to maintain this separation, ensuring that each layer has well-defined responsibilities and dependencies flow inward from the outer layers toward the core.

In short, Clean Architecture is not a one-size-fits-all solution, but it provides a solid framework for building Android apps that are maintainable, testable, and scalable. By adhering to its principles, you can create apps that stand the test of time, adapt to changing requirements, and remain robust in the face of evolving technologies. So, embrace the power of Clean Architecture and elevate your Android app development game to new heights. Your future self and your users will thank you for it.

Layers in Clean Architecture

Data Layer

In Clean Architecture for Android, the data layer plays a crucial role in managing the interaction between your application and external data sources, such as databases, web services, or repositories. The data layer is responsible for handling data storage, retrieval, and communication with these external sources, while keeping the core business logic of your application, located in the domain layer, agnostic of the data sources and their implementation details.

The data layer typically consists of the following components:

Repositories: Repositories are responsible for abstracting the details of data storage and retrieval. They define a set of methods that the use cases (interactors) in the domain layer can call to access data. Repositories act as a bridge between the domain layer and the actual data sources, shielding the domain layer from the specifics of how data is obtained or stored. In Android, repositories are often implemented using interfaces, and concrete implementations are provided using data sources.

Data Sources: Data sources are the concrete implementations responsible for interacting with external data providers, such as databases or web services. These can include local data sources (e.g., SQLite databases) and remote data sources (e.g., APIs). Data sources implement the methods defined in repositories to perform CRUD (Create, Read, Update, Delete) operations on data.

Mappers: Mappers are used to transform data between the format retrieved from data sources and the format expected by the domain layer. They help ensure that the data received from external sources is in a usable format for the domain layer entities and use cases. Mappers are particularly helpful when dealing with complex data transformations.

By structuring your Android application in this way, you achieve several benefits:

Separation of Concerns: Clean separation between the data layer and the domain layer ensures that the core business logic remains independent of data source-specific code.

Testability: The data layer can be tested independently of the Android framework, making it easier to write unit tests for your application.

Flexibility: You can replace or switch data sources without affecting the domain layer. For example, you could replace a local SQLite database with a remote API or vice versa.

Maintainability: Keeping data-related code isolated in the data layer makes it easier to maintain and extend your application as it evolves.

Overall, the data layer in Clean Architecture for Android provides a structured approach to managing data access and ensures that your application remains adaptable, maintainable, and testable in the face of changing requirements and data sources.

Domain Layer

In Clean Architecture for Android, the domain layer represents the core of your application's business logic and functionality. It is a central part of the architectural design that focuses on the core rules and operations of your app, independent of any external frameworks, databases, or user interfaces. The primary goal of the domain layer is to encapsulate and manage the core logic of your application in a way that is clean, maintainable, and agnostic to external dependencies.

Key characteristics and components of the domain layer in Clean Architecture for Android include:

Entities: Entities are at the heart of the domain layer. They represent the essential business objects or concepts within your application. These objects should have no knowledge of the database, UI, or any external framework. They are pure, framework-agnostic representations of your application's core data.

Use Cases (Interactors): Use cases, also known as interactors, are responsible for implementing the specific business rules and logic of your application. Each use case encapsulates a specific piece of functionality or a particular user story. They orchestrate the flow of data and operations within the domain layer. Use cases rely on entities to perform their tasks.

Repositories Interfaces: Repositories are defined as interfaces within the domain layer. They abstract the data access and storage operations needed by the use cases. Repositories declare methods that allow use cases to retrieve, save, or manipulate entities without needing to know where or how the data is stored. The actual implementation of repositories is provided in the data layer, which is responsible for interacting with external data sources.

Business Rules and Logic: The domain layer contains the core business rules, validation logic, and domain-specific algorithms that govern how your application behaves. This is where you enforce constraints, perform calculations, and validate user inputs based on the specific requirements of your domain.

Use Case Tests: In Clean Architecture, it is common practice to write unit tests for your use cases to ensure that the business logic functions correctly in isolation. Use case tests are typically independent of the Android framework and external dependencies, making them suitable for automated testing.

The domain layer serves as the innermost and most critical layer of Clean Architecture, encapsulating the core functionality and rules of your application. It is designed to be framework-agnostic, meaning it can be reused across different platforms, and it remains unaffected by changes in external technologies.

The benefits of the domain layer in Clean Architecture for Android include:

Maintainability: Separating the core business logic from external dependencies simplifies maintenance and updates.

Testability: The domain layer is highly testable, as it does not depend on Android-specific components. Unit tests can be written to ensure the correctness of business rules.

Flexibility: Changes to external frameworks, databases, or UI components do not require modifications to the domain layer, making it adaptable to evolving technology.

By implementing a robust domain layer, your Android application can achieve better separation of concerns, increased test coverage, improved maintainability, and greater flexibility in responding to changes in your app's requirements and external dependencies.

Presentation Layer

In Clean Architecture for Android, the presentation layer is the component responsible for handling the user interface (UI) and user interaction aspects of your application. It deals with the presentation and display of data to the user, as well as capturing and processing user input. The presentation layer plays a crucial role in creating a responsive and user-friendly experience while adhering to the principles of Clean Architecture.

Key characteristics and components of the presentation layer in Clean Architecture for Android include:

UI Components: The presentation layer includes all the user interface elements, such as activities, fragments, views, and widgets, that make up the visual part of your Android app. These components are responsible for rendering data to the user's screen and capturing user interactions, such as button clicks or text input.

View Models: In modern Android development, View Models play a central role in the presentation layer. They are responsible for storing and managing UI-related data, such as the state of the user interface, data to be displayed, and user inputs. View Models are particularly associated with the Model-View-ViewModel (MVVM) architectural pattern, which is commonly used in Android development.

Presenters: In the Model-View-Presenter (MVP) architectural pattern, presenters are used to separate the logic that controls the UI (presenter) from the Android-specific code (view). Presenters interact with the View (typically an Activity or Fragment) to update the UI and handle user input. This pattern aims to keep the UI as passive as possible.

UI Logic: The presentation layer contains UI-related logic, such as formatting data for display, handling user gestures, and managing navigation between different screens or fragments. This logic ensures a smooth and user-friendly experience while keeping the core business logic in the domain layer free from UI concerns.

Data Binding: Data binding libraries and frameworks, such as Android Data Binding, can be used in the presentation layer to establish a strong connection between UI elements and the underlying data. This helps reduce boilerplate code and simplifies the process of updating UI components with data changes.

UI Tests: The presentation layer is where you write UI tests to ensure that the user interface behaves as expected. UI tests can include both automated tests (e.g., Espresso tests) and manual testing to verify the user experience.

Dependencies on Domain Layer: The presentation layer depends on the domain layer for accessing business logic and use cases. It communicates with the domain layer through interfaces or abstractions defined in the domain layer, such as repositories and use cases.

The primary goals of the presentation layer are:

Separation of Concerns: Separating UI-related code from the core business logic (domain layer) ensures that each component has a well-defined responsibility, making the codebase more maintainable.

Testability: By following Clean Architecture principles, you can write unit tests for the presentation layer, including View Models or Presenters, to verify that UI-related logic functions correctly.

Adaptability: Changes to the user interface, such as redesigns or updates to UI components, can be made without affecting the core functionality of the app.

Overall, the presentation layer in Clean Architecture for Android is essential for creating a well-organised, testable, and adaptable user interface while keeping the core business logic of your application isolated from Android-specific concerns.

Significance of Clean Architecture in Android

Clean Architecture in Android is of significant importance because it provides a structured and well-defined approach to designing and organising Android applications. Here are some key reasons why Clean Architecture is significant in Android development:

Maintainability: Clean Architecture promotes a clear separation of concerns, with distinct layers for data, business logic, and presentation. This separation makes it easier to maintain and extend your Android app over time. Changes to one layer are less likely to ripple through the entire codebase, reducing the risk of introducing bugs during updates.

Testability: Clean Architecture encourages the creation of highly testable code. The separation of business logic from external dependencies allows for unit testing of core functionality without the need for Android-specific components. This leads to more reliable and robust applications.

Flexibility: Clean Architecture makes it easier to adapt your Android app to changing requirements, technologies, and external services. With well-defined boundaries between layers, you can replace or upgrade individual components without affecting the entire application. This adaptability is crucial in the fast-paced world of Android development.

Scalability: As your Android app grows and evolves, Clean Architecture provides a scalable foundation. You can add new features, modules, or external data sources without causing excessive complexity or dependencies. This scalability is essential for long-term app development.

Reduced Coupling: Clean Architecture reduces coupling between components and layers, making your codebase more modular. This modularity enables developers to work on different parts of the app in parallel and simplifies collaboration within development teams.

Technology Agnosticism: Clean Architecture encourages technology agnosticism, allowing you to switch out libraries, frameworks, or tools with minimal disruption to the overall architecture. This flexibility enables you to leverage the latest technologies and best practices.

Improved Code Quality: By adhering to Clean Architecture principles, you inherently improve the overall code quality of your Android app. The separation of concerns, clean code patterns, and adherence to SOLID principles lead to cleaner, more readable, and maintainable code.

User Interface Independence: Clean Architecture allows you to decouple the core business logic from the user interface. This means you can build multiple user interfaces (e.g., Android app, web app, desktop app) on top of the same core logic, maximizing code reuse.

Enhanced Collaboration: Clean Architecture fosters collaboration among development teams, designers, and stakeholders. It provides a clear architectural blueprint that helps everyone understand the structure and flow of the application.

Security and Stability: Clean Architecture promotes security by isolating sensitive data and logic in the domain layer. It also enhances stability by reducing the risk of unintended side effects when making changes to the codebase.

In summary, Clean Architecture is significant in Android development because it improves code maintainability, testability, flexibility, and scalability. It empowers developers to create robust, adaptable, and high-quality Android applications that can evolve with changing requirements and technological advancements. Clean Architecture serves as a solid foundation for building Android apps that stand the test of time.

Understanding MVVM Architecture

Introduction

In the world of Android app development, creating clean, maintainable, and testable code is essential. One architectural pattern that has gained widespread adoption for achieving these goals is MVVM, which stands for Model-View-ViewModel. MVVM separates an app into distinct layers, making it easier to manage complexity and build robust applications. In this chapter, we will explore what MVVM is, how it works, and its benefits in Android development.

What is MVVM

MVVM is an architectural design pattern that helps developers organise and structure Android applications. It encourages the separation of concerns by dividing an app into three main components: Model, View, and ViewModel.

1. Model:

The Model represents the data and business logic of the application. It encapsulates the data and operations related to that data. This can include data fetching from APIs, databases, or any other data source. Models are often implemented as data classes or repositories.

2. View:

The View is responsible for displaying the user interface and handling user interactions. In Android, Views are usually represented by XML layouts and activities/fragments. However, in MVVM, the View's role is limited to displaying data and forwarding user interactions to the ViewModel.

3. ViewModel:

The ViewModel acts as an intermediary between the Model and the View. It contains the presentation logic and exposes data that the View can observe and display. ViewModel instances survive configuration changes, ensuring that data remains intact when the device rotates or the app goes into the background.

How MVVM Works:

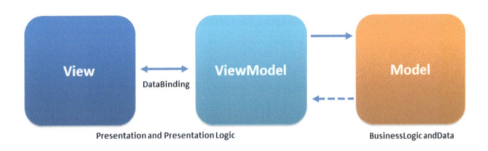

The core idea behind MVVM is data binding and the observability of data. Here's how MVVM works:

User Interaction: When a user interacts with the View (e.g., by clicking a button), the View forwards the interaction to the ViewModel.

ViewModel Updates: The ViewModel processes the user input, interacts with the Model to fetch or manipulate data, and updates its exposed data properties.

Data Binding: The View observes the data properties exposed by the ViewModel using data binding or other similar mechanisms. When the ViewModel updates these properties, the changes are automatically reflected in the View.

View Updates: The View, which is observing the ViewModel's data, automatically updates itself to reflect the changes in the ViewModel.

This two-way data flow ensures that the View and ViewModel stay synchronised without the need for complex callbacks or manual UI updates.

Benefits of MVVM:

MVVM offers several advantages in Android development:

Separation of Concerns: MVVM enforces a clear separation of concerns, making code easier to understand and maintain.

Testability: Because the ViewModel contains the presentation logic separate from the Android framework, it becomes highly testable. You can write unit tests for the ViewModel without dealing with UI components.

Reusability: ViewModel instances can be reused across different Views, promoting code reuse and reducing duplication.

Scalability: MVVM scales well for large and complex applications. As the project grows, MVVM's organisation and structure help manage complexity.

User Experience: MVVM can lead to a more responsive and user-friendly experience by allowing for efficient UI updates and reducing the risk of crashes due to configuration changes.

Story of MVVM

Once upon a time, in a magical land full of colourful widgets and talking smartphones, there lived a curious little Android named Hassan Shakoor. Hassan loved exploring the digital world and learning about all the amazing apps and games.

One sunny morning, as Hassan was playing with a friendly dragon game app, a wizard appeared on the screen. The wizard had a long, curly beard, and he wore a robe made of pixelated stars.

"Hello, young Android," the wizard said with a twinkle in his eye. "I see you're having fun, but do you want to learn something special today?"

Hassan Shakoor's eyes sparkled with excitement. "Yes, yes, please! What can you teach me, wise wizard?"

The wizard smiled and waved his magic wand, and suddenly, Hassan found himself inside a colourful, pixelated castle. It was the magical kingdom of MVVM, where everything was organised, just like a neat and tidy toy chest.

"Welcome to MVVM-land!" the wizard exclaimed. "Here, we have three special friends: Model, View, and ViewModel. They work together to create fantastic apps."

Model was a diligent worker who collected all the information Hassan needed. He knew the weather, the news, and even the latest cat videos. Model had a giant book with all the data.

View was the artistic friend. She took the information from Model's book and drew beautiful pictures on a giant canvas. Whenever Hassan wanted to see something, View would show it to him.

ViewModel was the messenger. He ran between Model and View, carrying the data and pictures back and forth. He made sure everything was in the right place at the right time.

The wizard explained, "With MVVM, we can make amazing apps by keeping things organised. Model holds the data, View makes it look pretty, and ViewModel helps them talk to each other. And best of all, it's easy for you, little Android, to understand!"

Hassan was thrilled to learn about MVVM. He realised that it was like building a digital playhouse, with each friend doing their part to make everything fun and beautiful.

The wizard waved his wand again, and Hassan returned to his game. This time, he saw the game's code was organised just like the MVVM-land castle. It was neat, efficient, and made Hassan's dragon adventure even more exciting.

From that day on, Hassan knew the magic of MVVM. Whenever he created his own apps, he remembered Model, View, and ViewModel, and how they worked together like the best team in the world. And just like that, Hassan became one of the best Android app creators in the magical land of the digital kingdom.

And so, with the wisdom of MVVM in his heart, Hassan continued to explore the wondrous world of Android, sharing his knowledge with other little Androids along the way. The end, my dear friend!

Conclusion:

MVVM (Model-View-ViewModel) is a powerful architectural pattern that helps Android developers create well-structured, maintainable, and testable applications. By separating concerns and enabling efficient data binding, MVVM simplifies the development process while improving the overall user experience. Whether you're building a simple app or a complex one, MVVM is a valuable pattern to consider for your Android development projects.

Mastering MVI (Model-View-Intent)

Creating apps that are not only feature-rich but also maintainable, scalable, and bug-free is a daunting challenge. That's where architectural patterns come to the rescue. One such pattern that has gained traction in recent years is the Model-View-Intent (MVI) architecture. In this article, we will delve into the MVI pattern, explore its principles, and understand how it can help you build better Android apps.

Understanding MVI

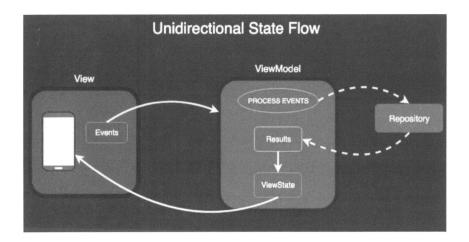

MVI stands for Model-View-Intent, and it offers a clear and structured way to develop Android applications. At its core, MVI is designed to achieve two primary goals:

Unidirectional Data Flow: MVI enforces a one-way data flow in the application. This means that data flows in a single direction, from the Model to the View, with well-defined stops in between.

Immutable State: MVI promotes the use of immutable data structures for representing the application's state. Any changes to the state result in the creation of a new state object rather than modifying the existing one.

Key Components of MVI

To better understand MVI, let's break down its key components:

Model (M): The Model represents the application's state and business logic. It holds all the data that the application needs to function correctly. In MVI, the Model is entirely responsible for managing the state and ensuring its immutability.

View (V): The View is responsible for displaying the user interface and presenting data to the user. However, it does not directly interact with the Model. Instead, the View observes changes to the state and reacts accordingly.

Intent (I): The Intent represents user actions, interactions, or events that can trigger a state change. It serves as a bridge between the user's actions and the Model. Intents are typically expressed as immutable objects or events.

Example

Imagine you're building a robot that can talk to people and do tasks. In MVI, your robot has three parts:

Brain (Model): This is like the robot's memory and decision-maker. It stores all the information the robot needs, like what it knows about the world and what it's supposed to do.

Eyes and Ears (View): These are like the robot's senses. They help the robot see and hear what's happening in the world, which is what the robot shows to people.

Mouth and Hands (Intent): These are like the robot's way of communicating and doing things. When someone talks to the robot or gives it a task, the robot listens to them (Intent) and then decides what to do (Brain).

Here's how it works:

Someone Talks (User Interaction): Imagine a person talks to the robot or gives it a task, like "Tell me the weather" or "Turn on the lights."

Listening and Understanding (Intent): The robot's "Ears and Eyes" listen and understand what the person is saying. They create a message (Intent) that tells the robot what the person wants.

Making Decisions (Model): The robot's "Brain" takes that message (Intent) and decides what to do. For example, if the person asked about the weather, the Brain figures out the weather and what to say.

Talking and Doing (View): Finally, the robot's "Mouth and Hands" (View) show or tell the person what the robot has decided to do. For instance, it might say, "The weather is sunny," or it could turn on the lights.

Repeat: The robot keeps listening, deciding, and doing things as long as people talk to it.

The great thing about MVI is that it makes the robot's actions easy to understand, test, and change. It also helps the robot stay organised and not get confused.

So, MVI is like giving your robot a smart brain (Model), sharp senses (View), and clear communication skills (Intent) to help it do tasks and talk to people in an orderly and efficient way. It's like teaching your robot to be a super helper!

Comparing MVVM, Clean architecture and MVI

Comparing Clean Architecture, MVVM (Model-View-ViewModel), and MVI (Model-View-Intent) in Android can help you understand their differences and when to use each pattern. Here's a comparison of these three architectural approaches:

1. Clean Architecture:

Key Principles:

Separation of concerns: Divides the app into distinct layers: Domain, Data, and Presentation.

Dependency Inversion: High-level modules depend on abstractions, not concrete implementations.

Testability: Emphasises unit testing, as business logic is isolated in the Domain layer.

Pros:

Highly modular and maintainable.

Testable, with clear boundaries for unit testing.

Supports domain-driven design.

Encourages SOLID principles.

Cons:

Can be complex for small projects.

Initial setup and learning curve can be steep.

Requires careful planning and design.

When to Use:

Recommended for large, complex apps with multiple features and a long lifecycle.

Projects where a strong focus on architecture and maintainability is essential.

2. MVVM (Model-View-ViewModel):

Key Principles:

Separation of concerns: Separates UI logic from business logic.

Data Binding: Often used with data binding libraries to bind UI elements directly to ViewModel properties.

Lifecycle Awareness: ViewModel is lifecycle-aware and survives configuration changes.

Pros:

Clear separation of concerns.

Easily testable, especially when combined with LiveData or RxJava.

Well-suited for applications with complex UIs.

Compatible with Android Jetpack components.

Cons:

Requires a deeper understanding of Android's architecture components.

Can introduce a learning curve for new developers.

When to Use:

Suitable for a wide range of Android applications, from medium to large in size.

Ideal for projects that require data synchronisation between the UI and backend.

3. MVI (Model-View-Intent):

Key Principles:

Unidirectional data flow: Enforces a one-way flow of data, which simplifies app behaviour.

Immutable state: Encourages the use of immutable data structures to represent the app's state.

Intent-driven: User interactions are translated into intents, which dictate state changes.

Pros:

Predictable and testable due to unidirectional data flow.

Easier debugging and error tracing.

Scalable for complex applications with a predictable UI.

Cons:

Learning curve, especially for developers new to reactive programming.

May introduce additional complexity for simpler apps.

When to Use:

Recommended for applications that prioritise predictability and testability.

Suitable for complex applications where managing app state is a challenge.

Choosing the Right Architecture

Before selecting an architecture, thoroughly understand your app's requirements, goals, and constraints. Consider factors such as:

App complexity: Is your app simple or complex?

Team expertise: What architectural patterns are your team members familiar with?

Project timeline: How much time do you have for development?

Performance and scalability: Do you expect a large user base?

Here are some general guidelines:

Clean Architecture

Best suited for large, complex apps where long-term maintainability is a top priority and you need strict separation of concerns.

MVVM

A versatile choice for a wide range of Android apps, especially when using Android Jetpack components and when you want to simplify UI logic.

MVI

Ideal for applications that require a high level of predictability, testability, and maintainability, particularly in complex scenarios with many user interactions and state changes.

In practice, many projects may even combine elements of these architectures to tailor the solution to their specific needs. Ultimately, the choice of architecture should align with the project's goals and constraints while considering the team's familiarity with the chosen pattern.

Final Notes

As we reach the final pages of this book, I want to extend my heartfelt thanks to you, dear reader, for embarking on this architectural journey with me. Throughout this book, we've explored the intricate world of Android app architecture, delving into practices that not only make your apps more robust but also elevate your development skills.

I hope this book has been more than just a guide; I hope it's been a companion, providing you with insights and knowledge that will empower you in your Android development endeavours. Remember, architecture is not just about coding; it's about crafting sustainable solutions that stand the test of time.

The Path Forward

As you close this book and perhaps set it aside for a moment, I encourage you to reflect on your newfound wisdom. The architectural principles you've discovered here are not the end but the beginning of your journey toward becoming a more adept Android developer.

The Android ecosystem is continually evolving, and the world of app architecture evolves with it. Stay curious, keep learning, and embrace new technologies and practices as they emerge. Your commitment to learning is what sets you apart as a developer.

A Call to Action

Now, it's time for action. Implement the best practices you've learned in your projects, experiment with different architectural patterns, and fine-tune your skills. Don't hesitate to seek out help from the vibrant Android developer community; we're all here to support each other's growth.

Remember that architecture is a tool, not a burden. It's there to make your life easier, your code more maintainable, and your apps more user-friendly. Embrace it with enthusiasm, and you'll find that it can be one of your most valuable assets.

Thank You

Once again, I want to express my gratitude for joining me on this educational journey. Your commitment to mastering Android app architecture speaks volumes about your dedication to your craft. I wish you the very best in all your future Android development projects and endeavours.

Stay passionate, stay curious, and keep building remarkable Android apps that make a positive impact on the world.

With warm regards,

Syed Ahmad Shahwaiz

www.ingramcontent.com/pod-product-compliance
Lightning Source LLC
La Vergne TN
LVHW060159050326
832903LV00017B/363